Wriggle and Roar!

Rhymes to join in with

by Julia Donaldson

illustrated by Nick Sharratt

MACMILLAN CHILDREN'S BOOKS

For Melody – J.D.
For Lily, Lucy and Florence – N.S.

First published in 2004 by Macmillan Children's Books
a division of Macmillan Publishers Limited
20 New Wharf Road, London N1 9RR
Basingstoke and Oxford
Associated companies worldwide
www.panmacmillan.com

ISBN 1 405 02165 9 (HB)
ISBN 1 405 02166 7 (PB)

Text copyright © 2004 Julia Donaldson
Illustrations copyright © 2004 Nick Sharratt
Moral rights asserted.

3 5 7 9 8 6 4 2 (HB)
1 3 5 7 9 8 6 4 2 (PB)

A CIP catalogue record for this book is available from the British Library.

Printed in Belgium by Proost

Contents

Animal Voices

Can you . . .

PURR like a cat in the sun?
SQUEAK like a mouse on the run?

GRUNT like a pig in a sty?
TWEET like a bird in the sky?

BAA like a sheep in a pen?
CLUCK like an egg-laying hen?

BUZZ like a bumbly bee?
CAW like a crow in a tree?

CHOMP like a horse with a carrot?
SHRIEK like a red and green parrot?

The Terrible Tickle

I've got a little tickle
In between my toes.
Tickle, tickle, off you go!
Away the tickle goes.

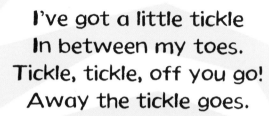

Now that little tickle
Is tickling my knee.
Tickle, tickle, off you go!
Don't you tickle me!

That silly little tickle
Is tickling my tum.
Tickle, tickle, off you go,
Or I'll tell my mum.

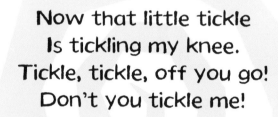

That naughty little tickle
Has jumped behind my ear.
Tickle, tickle, off you go!
Stop it, do you hear!

That terror of a tickle
Is tickling my nose.
Tickle, tickle, off you go!
It's GONE . . .
        back to my toes!

Toenails

One, two, three, four, five, six, seven,
Eight, nine, ten.
I've coloured all my toenails with a
Felt-tipped pen.
Now I'll have to scrub until they're
Clean again.
One, two, three, four, five, six, seven,
Eight, nine, ten.

How Does Your Garden Grow?

The very first thing that a gardener needs
Is a hoe for pulling up all the weeds.
So here we go, a-hoeing-o,
Hoeing the garden to make it grow.

A spade comes next, for digging the earth.
Let's dig and shovel for all we're worth.
So here we go, a-digging-o,
Digging the garden to make it grow.

Put down the spade. Pick up a rake
And rake it smooth as a crumbly cake.
So here we go, a-raking-o,
Raking the garden to make it grow.

We've raked, we've dug, we've weeded the ground.
It's time to scatter some seeds around.
So here we go, a-sowing-o,
Sowing the garden to make it grow.

Those seeds are feeling thirsty, I think.
We'd better give them a nice long drink.
So here we go, a-watering-o,
Watering the garden to make it grow.

Nod, Shake, Shrug

Would you like a currant bun?
Are tomatoes red?
That's the kind of question
That makes me nod my head.

Would you like to tidy up?
Is it time for bed?
That's the kind of question
That makes me shake my head.

Would you rather crunch a snail
Or gobble up a slug?
That's the kind of question
That makes my shoulders shrug.

13

One, two, three, BLOW!

Three red candles
In a row.
One, two, three,

BLOW!

Three brown biscuits,
Much too high.
One, two, three,

SIGH!

Goldilocks

Goldilocks tasted three bowls of porridge.

Goldilocks sat on three kitchen chairs.

Goldilocks lay on three feather pillows.

Goldilocks ran – from three angry bears!
Grrrrr, GRRRRRRR, GRRRRRRRRRRRRRRR!

Snakes

Snake, snake, sleepy snake.
Sleepy snake won't hiss.

Snake, snake, wide awake,
Hisses just like . . .
thissssssssssssssssssssss!

Nut Tree

Small, brown, hard, round,
The nut is lying underground.

Now a shoot begins to show.
Now the shoot begins to grow.

Tall, taller, tall as can be,
The shoot is growing into a tree.

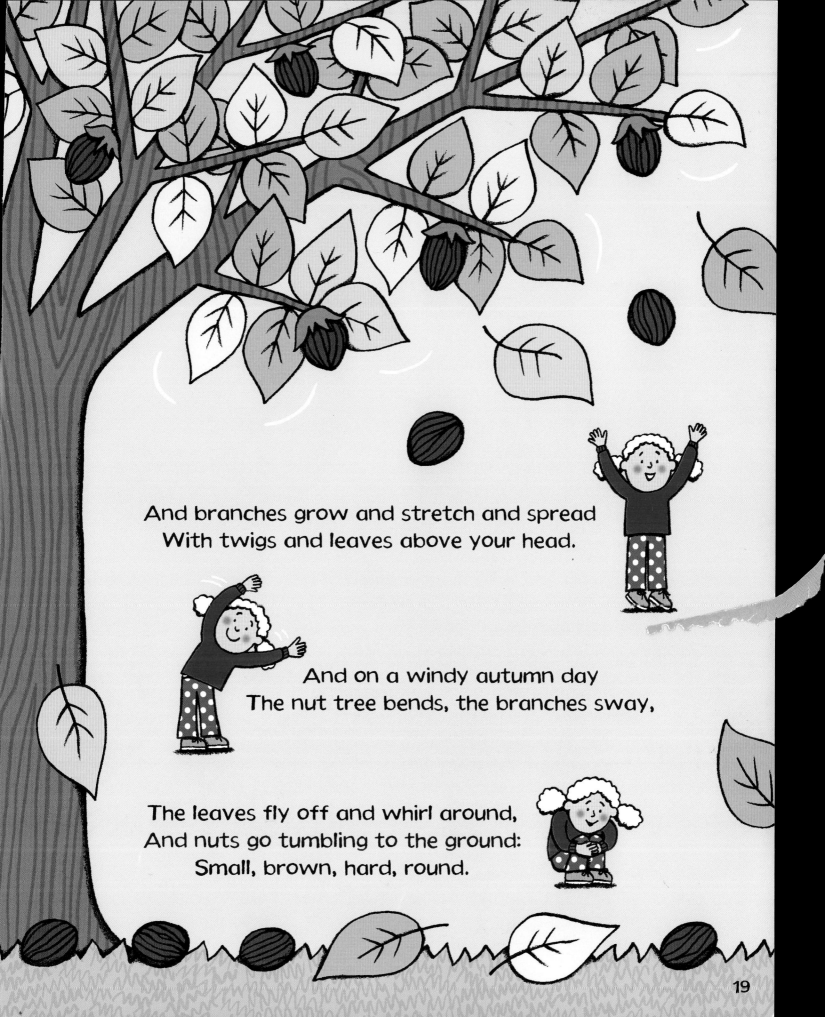

And branches grow and stretch and spread
With twigs and leaves above your head.

And on a windy autumn day
The nut tree bends, the branches sway,

The leaves fly off and whirl around,
And nuts go tumbling to the ground:
Small, brown, hard, round.

Birdsong

Deep in the wood I heard a bird:
Too-whit, too-whoo.
I said to the woodland bird I heard,
"And who are you?"
"I am an owl, a woodland owl,
How do you do, too-whoo?
Too-whit, too-whoo."

Down by the sea I heard a bird:
Mee-ew, mee-ew.
I said to the seaside bird I heard,
"And who are you?"
"I am a gull, a seaside gull,
How do you do, mee-ew?
Mee-ew, mee-ew."

Out in the country I heard a bird:
Cuckoo, cuckoo.
I said to the country bird I heard,
"And who are you?"
"I am a cuckoo, a country cuckoo,
How do you do, cuckoo?
Cuckoo, cuckoo."

Down on the farm I heard a bird:
Cock-a-doodledoo.
I said to the farmyard bird I heard,
"Who on earth are you?"
"I am a cock, a farmyard cock,
How do you doodledoo?
Cock-a-doodledoo."

Too-whit, too-whoo,
Mee-ew, mee-ew,
Cuckoo, cuckoo,
Cock-a-doodledoo!

Sniff, Sniff, Sniff

Sniff, sniff, sniff.
What can you sniff?
A lump of cheese all covered in mould,
Looking about a hundred years old,
That's what I can sniff.

Sniff, sniff, sniff.
What can you sniff?
A nasty, mouldy, rotten old veg,
Soggy inside and fluffy round the edge,
That's what I can sniff.

Sniff, sniff, sniff.
What can you sniff?
A pair of socks that never have been
Anywhere near a washing machine,
That's what I can sniff.

Handy Work

One, two,
What can you do?
We can . . .

Stroke a cat,
Put on a hat,

Shake your hand,
Dig in the sand,

Drive a car,
Play the guitar,

Scrub the floor,
Knock on the door,

Turn a screw,
Tie up a shoe,

Toot the flute,
Pull off a boot,

Brush your hair,
Cuddle a bear,

Wave goodnight
And switch out the light.

Quick! Quick! Hang Out Your Washing

Quick! Quick! Hang out your washing!
Hang it all out on the line.
The sky is blue and the clouds are white
And the sun has begun to shine.
The sun will dry your stripy socks,
Trousers and blouses and party frocks,
So, quick! Quick! Hang them all out,
Hang them all out on the line.

Quick! Quick! Take in your washing!
Take it all in from the line.
The sky is grey and the clouds are black
And the weather is far from fine.
The rain will soak your stripy socks,
Trousers and blouses and party frocks,
So, quick! Quick! Take them all in,
Take them all in from the line.

29

Two Feet

Two feet,
Tapping out a beat.

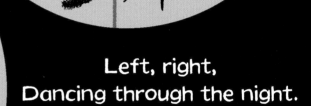

Left, right,
Dancing through the night.

Tip-toe,
Creeping to and fro.

Leap, jump,
Landing with a thump.

Two feet,
Stamping down the street.

Left, right,
Running out of sight.

31

Shhhhhhh!

Shhhhhhh!
Don't rushhh,
Or the fox will be off
With a swishhh
Of its brushhh.

Hushhh!
Don't splashhh,
Or the shhhimmering fishhh
Will be gone in a flashhh.

Shushhh!
Don't crashhh,
Or the shhhy thrushhh
That sings in the bushhh
Will vanishhh.
The song
Will
Finishhhhhhhh.

32